MILITARY QUOTAT

Military quotations
for managers

Mick Verbrugge & Tim Royall

SeevanckPublishers

© copyright Seevanck Publishers 2015

Edited by Les Glazier
Cover and typeset by Marco Bolsenbroek
Illustrations by Frans Reijers

All rights reserved. No part of this publication may be reproduced, stored in or introduced into a retrieval system, or transmitted, in any form (print, photocopy, electronic or otherwise), or by any means, without the prior written permission of the publisher. Any person who does any unauthorised act in relation to this publication may be liable to criminal prosecution and civil claims for damages.

ISBN-13: 978-9-081-638180

While best efforts have been used in preparing this book, the author and publisher make no representations or warranties of any kind and assume no liabilities of any kind with respect to the accuracy or completeness of the contents and specifically disclaim any implied warranties of merchantability or fitness of use for a particular purpose. Every effort has been made to fulfil the requirements with regard to reproducing copyright material but if any have been inadvertently overlooked, the publisher will be pleased to make the necessary arrangements at the first opportunity.

British Library Cataloguing-in-Publication Data
A catalogue record of this book is available from the British Library.

Seevanck Publishers books are available as special editions to use as sales promotions. For more information, please contact us at sales@seevanck.com or look at our website.

Printed and bound in Europe.

Content

Introduction	7
1. Generals and leadership	11
2. Planning and strategy	33
3. The battlefield and marketplace	55
4. Officers and management	69
5. Army and careers	89
6. Soldiers and employees	113
7. Victory and financial success	143
The generals and warlords	159
Sources and accountability	174
Other titles in this series	176

Introduction

Since the beginning of mankind, we have gone to war against each other. Wars have been inspired by such feelings as power, honour, ideology, and megalomania, and have often resulted in large, but temporary, empires such as those of the Greeks, Romans, French, Mongols or British. Fighting wars has long been seen as an 'art'. It has also led to many advances in technology and developments in the manner of organization and planning, leading to many insights and principles that are relevant to all kinds of businesses and organizations today.

Generals and warlords

This book features more than thirty of the world's most famous generals and warlords who all have a claim to fame and who have played a militarily important role in their time – generals and warlords who have nearly all seen action in the front line. And while every country has its own famous general or warlord from history, making a global choice has proved a much more difficult task. No quotations have been included in this book from General von Clausewitz (1780-1831), who is praised in military circles for his insights and whose book Von Krieg still serves as a benchmark for military and political strategy. This is because he was a military theorist rather than a general in the front line.

Quotes as an inspiration

Famous people are often remembered as much for the things they said as for their actions, and the same applies to the generals and warlords. This book presents nearly five hundred quotations – short and powerful quotations – whose meaning is both immediately clear and relevant in today's business world. The quotations themselves are either directly from the generals or attributed to them by tradition.

The military quotations in this book are organized according to seven management topics: leadership, strategy, commerce, management, staff, employees, and finance. Within each management topic, there is a further breakdown by sub-topic such as image, sales, career, character, and results. Each quotation is accompanied by the name of the general or warlord to whom it is attributed. More information about the generals or warlords can be found at the back of the book.

Practical and fun

Managers who want to strengthen their message or presentation with a suitable quotation will find plenty of inspiration in this book. As Frederick the Great once said, 'The spirit is easily persuaded when the heart is stirred'.

CHAPTER 1.
Generals and leadership

In most countries, a four-star General is the highest military rank in the army and the air force. The equivalent rank in the navy is Admiral. Some countries have higher ranks such as Field Marshal or five-star General. A General is normally responsible for combined formations of units such as infantry, armour, artillery, engineers and support services such as communications and medical services. This chapter takes a closer look at particular leadership qualities such as initiative, the ability to inspire, confidence and endurance.

TAKING THE LEAD

There is nothing impossible to him who will try

Alexander the Great

If your sword is too short, take one step forward

Marquis Heihachiro Togo

I am convinced that life is 10% what happens to me and 96% how I react to it!

Scipio Africanus

People who hesitate have little success in their affairs

Napoleon Bonaparte

Lead me, follow me, or get out of my way

George Patton Jr

Leading is done forward

Erwin Rommel

REPUTATION

Reputation is everything that is left us after death

Frederick the Great

A tomb now suffices for him for whom the whole world was not sufficient

Alexander the Great

All glory is fleeting

George Patton Jr

Death is nothing, but to live defeated and inglorious is to die daily

Napoleon Bonaparte

Men of genius are meteors destined to burn to light their century

Napoleon Bonaparte

Success is how high you bounce after you hit bottom

George Patton Jr

Posterity alone, which is aimed without passion and self-interest, can condemn us

Frederick the Great

The titles are only ornaments for the silly; big men just need their names

Frederick the Great

I am not carrying on a war
of extermination against the
Romans. I am contending for
honour and empire. My ancestors
yielded to Roman valour. I am
endeavouring that others, in
their turn, will be obliged to
yield to my good fortune, and my
valour

Hannibal

You cannot be buried in
obscurity: you are exposed
upon a grand stage to the view
of the world. If your actions
are upright and benevolent, be
assured they will augment your
power and happiness

Cyrus the Great

If the nation only knew their hands dripped with innocent blood, it would have met them not with applause but with stones

Georgy Zhukov

I used to say of him [Napoleon] that his presence on the field made the difference of forty thousand men

Duke of Wellington

The pursuit of lasting fame is the most powerful and chief driving force of the soul. It is the source and the reason for which men are driven to virtue and from which arises all the acts by which they make themselves immortal

Frederick the Great

My character and good name are in my own keeping. Life with disgrace is dreadful. A glorious death is to be envied

Horatio Nelson

Associate yourself with men of good quality if you esteem your own reputation for 'tis better to be alone than in bad company

George Washington

CONFIDENCE

My trust is in the mercy and wisdom of a kind providence, who ordereth all things for our good

Robert E. Lee

All very successful commanders are prima donnas and must be so treated

George Patton Jr

Hold one hand out in friendship, but keep the other on your sword

Saladin

The reliance on one's own strength is the foundation of all bravery!

Frederick the Great

Hard pounding, gentlemen. Let's see who pounds the longest

Duke of Wellington

Where you find Zhukov, there you find victory

Georgy Zhukov

In war, he who doubts is lost: we must never doubt

Ferdinand Foch

A leader is a dealer in hope

Napoleon Bonaparte

As Lord Chesterfield said of the generals of his day, I only hope that when the enemy reads the list of their names, he trembles as I do

Duke of Wellington

The German army is the sword of the new world

Erwin Rommel

If we come to a minefield, our infantry attacks exactly as if it were not there

Georgy Zhukov

LEADERSHIP QUALITIES

Leadership is the art of getting someone else to do something you want done because he wants to do it

Dwight D. Eisenhower

A leader is a man who can adapt principles to circumstances

George Patton Jr

The general who advances without coveting fame and retreats without fearing disgrace, whose only thought is to protect his country and do good service for his sovereign, is the jewel of the kingdom

Sun Tzu

The forbearing use of power does not only form a touchstone, but the manner in which an individual enjoys certain advantages over others is a test of a true gentleman

Robert E. Lee

Leadership is a potent combination of strategy and character. But if you must be without one, be without strategy

H. Norman Schwarzkopf

Leadership is the capacity and will to rally men and women to a common purpose and the character which inspires confidence

Montgomery

Stamina, tolerance, persistence!

Frederick the Great

If you leave here with the word
DUTY implanted in your mind; if
you leave here with the word
HONOUR carved in your soul; if
you leave here with a love of
COUNTRY stamped on your heart,
then you will be a worthy
twenty-first century leader

H. Norman Schwarzkopf

There's a great deal of talk
about loyalty from the bottom
to the top. Loyalty from the top
down is even more necessary and
is much less prevalent.

George Patton Jr

He who turns to the imagination
of the people will always defeat
those who want to act on their
minds

Frederick the Great

I am the punishment of God... If you had not committed great sins, God would not have sent a punishment like me upon you

Genghis Khan

Heaven cannot brook two suns, nor earth two masters

Alexander the Great

Great men are not always large and not in all things

Frederick the Great

Regard your soldiers as your children, and they will follow you into the deepest valleys. Look on them as your own beloved sons, and they will stand by you even unto death!

Sun Tzu

HEROISM

It doesn't take a hero to order men into battle. It takes a hero to be one of those men who goes into battle

H. Norman Schwarzkopf

In honour I gained them*, and in honour I will die with them
(*the stars on his uniform)

Horatio Nelson

If you're afraid - don't do it, if you're doing it - don't be afraid!

Genghis Khan

The only thing I am afraid of is fear

Duke of Wellington

Zhukov was the only person who feared no one. He was not even afraid of Stalin

Georgy Zhukov

Which death is preferable to every other? The unexpected

Julius Caesar

COMPASSION

All should be free to worship their God without harm... No one's home [may] be destroyed and no one's property be looted

Cyrus the Great

The so-called good fighting generals of the war appeared to me to be those who had a complete disregard for human life. There were of course exceptions and I suppose one was Plumer*
(*British Field Marshal Herbert Plumer)

Montgomery

A king does not kill a king

Saladin

It is a weakness, even narrow-mindedness, not to say good of your enemies, and not to allow them the justice they deserve

Frederick the Great

Next to a lost battle, nothing is so sad as a battle that has been won

Duke of Wellington

How do we get people to hatch big plans which cost so much blood? We want to live and let live!

Frederick the Great

Look after your people and they will bless you: that is the true glory

Frederick the Great

ENDURANCE

Against fate only one thing helps me: steadfastness

Frederick the Great

Accept the challenges so that you can feel the exhilaration of victory

George Patton Jr

God grant me the courage not to give up what I think is right, even though I think it is hopeless

Chester W. Nimitz

Prussian field marshals do not mutiny

Erich von Manstein

CHAPTER 2.
Planning and strategy

Military strategy is all about the preparation for taking part in warfare. Within the military, people use the following terms to describe operations: tactics are the general/lower-level ways of actually conducting warfare on the ground while the strategy, or strategic plans, generally concern, or are linked to, policy decisions at the highest level. This chapter looks at strategic issues such as the mission, planning, implementation and control.

MISSION

With God's help I have conquered a huge empire for you. But my life was too short to achieve the conquest of the world. That task is left for you

Genghis Khan

I have never advocated war except as a means of peace

Ulysses S. Grant

We will do all we can to ensure peace... but if war is imposed upon us, we will be together, shoulder to shoulder, as in the last war to strive for the happiness of mankind

Georgy Zhukov

Our cause is noble; it is the cause of mankind!

George Washington

The worst way one can choose is to choose no way at all

Frederick the Great

The whole art of war consists of getting at what is on the other side of the hill

Duke of Wellington

STRATEGIC THINKING

Win with ability, not with numbers

Aleksandr Vasilyevich Suvorov

When we are fighting there is no need to think of defence. A perfect attack is the best form of defence

Marquis Heihachiro Togo

A defensive policy involves the loss of the initiative, with all the consequent disadvantages to the defender

Douglas Haig

War is an art and as such is not susceptible to explanation by a fixed formula

George Patton Jr

If everyone is thinking alike, someone isn't thinking

George Patton Jr

A prince who listens to advice is also capable of following it

Frederick the Great

Read history, works of truth, not novels and romances

Robert E. Lee

From the sublime to the ridiculous there is only one short step

Napoleon Bonaparte

Anyone can have knowledge but the art of being able to think about it is the rarest gift of nature

Frederick the Great

We should not look back unless it is to derive useful lessons from past errors, and for the purpose of profiting by dearly bought experience

George Washington

To fight and win all your battles is not supreme excellence; supreme excellence consists of breaking the enemy's resistance without fighting

Sun Tzu

PLANNING

Plans are nothing; planning is everything.

Dwight D. Eisenhower

A good plan executed today is better than a perfect plan executed at some indefinite point in the future

George Patton Jr

The victorious strategist only seeks battle after the victory has been won, whereas he who is destined to defeat first fights and afterwards looks for victory

Sun Tzu

A battle is fought by logistic experts before it actually starts

Erwin Rommel

It is easier to make our wishes conform to our means than to make our means conform to our wishes

Robert E. Lee

It is unfortunate when final decisions are made by chieftains headquartered miles away from the front, where they can only guess at conditions and possibilities known only to the leader on the battlefield

Atilla the Hun

It is always a bad thing if
political considerations
are allowed to influence the
planning of operations

Erwin Rommel

Many things which nature makes
difficult become easy to the man
who uses his brains

Hannibal

The business of the English
commander-in-chief being first
to bring an enemy fleet to
battle on the most advantageous
terms to himself, (I mean that of
laying his ships close on board
the enemy, as expeditiously
as possible); and secondly to
continue them there until the
business is decided

Horatio Nelson

The art of war teaches us not to rely on the likelihood of the enemy not coming, but on our own readiness to receive him; not on the chance of his not attacking, but rather on the fact that we have made our position unassailable

Sun Tzu

Although we have heard that haste is seldom good in war, long delays have also never been been associated with cleverness

Sun Tzu

It is only by doing things others have not that one can advance

George Patton Jr

The vital point in actual warfare is to apply to the enemy what we do not wish to be applied to ourselves and at the same time not to let the enemy apply it to us. Therefore, it is most important that we consider what would embarrass them before they can do the same to us; we must always forestall them

Marquis Heihachiro Togo

Give the enemy not only a route to flee, but also a reason to defend that route

Scipio Africanus

EXECUTION

If your men fear you, they will fight for you. But if they like you, they will die for you!

Napoleon Bonaparte

The art of war is a simple art and everything revolves around the execution. Everything is common sense, nothing is ideology

Napoleon Bonaparte

We will either find a way, or make one

Hannibal

Experience is the teacher of all things

Julius Caesar

Something must be left to chance; nothing is certain in a sea fight

Horatio Nelson

We must lose our arrogance, and we should act, not philosophize

Frederick the Great

Gentlemen, when the enemy is committed to a mistake we must not interrupt him too soon

Horatio Nelson

Go forward until the last round is fired and the last drop of gas is expended... then go forward on foot!

George Patton Jr

I cannot command the winds and weather

Horatio Nelson

In making tactical dispositions, the highest that you can achieve is to conceal them

Sun Tzu

My troops may fail to take a position, but are never driven from one!

Thomas 'Stonewall' Jackson

Move not unless you see an advantage; use not your troops unless there is something to be gained; fight not unless the position is critical. If it is to your advantage, make a forward move; if not, stay where you are

Sun Tzu

Never break the neutrality of a port or place, but never consider as neutral any place from whence an attack is allowed to be made

Horatio Nelson

The march to Jerusalem will not be delayed, for this is precisely the right time to liberate it

Saladin

I will start with conquest. Scholars will acknowledge me later that I was right

Frederick the Great

If we had not driven them into hell, hell would have swallowed us

Aleksandr Vasilyevich Suvorov

Strength comes from resistance against misfortune

Frederick the Great

It goes well, the mountain has been bypassed

Frederick the Great

Though force can protect in emergency, only justice, fairness, consideration and cooperation can finally lead men to the dawn of eternal peace

Dwight D. Eisenhower

When the enemy is driven back, we have failed, and when he is cut off, encircled and dispersed, we have succeeded

Aleksandr Vasilyevich Suvorov

There is only one tactical principle which is not subject to change. It is to use the means at hand to inflict the maximum amount of wounds, death, and destruction on the enemy in the minimum amount of time

George Patton Jr

Here they found real war, but they were not ready for it. They were used to easy victories. This deprived them of flexibility on the one hand, of tenacity on the other. For them, war was merely manoeuvres.

Georgy Zhukov

REORGANIZATION

All motion is relative. Perhaps it is you who have moved away by standing still

Robert E. Lee

Make your plans to fit the circumstances

George Patton Jr

War is cruelty. There's no use trying to reform it, the crueller it is the sooner it will be over

William Tecumseh Sherman

It is easier to find men who will volunteer to die than to find those who are willing to endure pain with patience

Julius Caesar

Air power is indivisible. If you split it up into compartments, you merely pull it to pieces and destroy its greatest asset, its flexibility

Montgomery

The great art is to change during the battle. Woe to the general who comes to fight with a system

Napoleon Bonaparte

CRISIS MANAGEMENT

Once the mass of the defending infantry become possessed of low morale, the battle is as good as lost

Douglas Haig

To accept the idea of defeat is to be defeated

Ferdinand Foch

The turning points of lives are not the great moments. The real crises are often concealed in occurrences so trivial in appearance that they pass unobserved

George Washington

My centre is giving way, my right is in retreat. An ideal situation, I am attacking

Ferdinand Foch

Every position must be held to the last man: there must be no rest. With our backs to the wall, and believing in the justice of our cause, each one of us must fight on until the end

Douglas Haig

CHAPTER 3.

The battlefield and marketplace

A battle is a clash between enemy armies. Originally it would take place in open spaces, often at a mutually agreed location, and the land on which it took place was called the battlefield. Carl von Clausewitz said that the employment of battles to achieve the object of war was the essence of strategy. Companies today often describe their aproach to business in military terms, comparing the marketplace to a battlefield. In the same vein, this chapter also covers areas such as marketing, sales, competition and cooperation.

MARKETS AND MARKETING

Men are nearly always willing to believe what they wish

Julius Caesar

Without a doubt, psychological warfare has proven its right to a place of dignity in our military arsenal

Dwight D. Eisenhower

If we do go to war, psychological operations are going to be absolutely a critical, critical part of any campaign that we must get involved in

H. Norman Schwarzkopf

One cannot wage war under present conditions without the support of public opinion, which is tremendously moulded by the press and other forms of propaganda

Douglas MacArthur

Public morality is the natural complement of all laws: it is an entire code in itself

Napoleon Bonaparte

The spirit is easily persuaded when the heart is stirred

Frederick the Great

Few people think, but everyone can be touched by the simple story of an event

Frederick the Great

In general, all evils which are distant alarm men's minds most powerfully

Julius Caesar

Official journals must not be generated

Frederick the Great

I fear three newspapers more than 100,000 bayonets

Napoleon Bonaparte

INNOVATION

There never was a time when, in my opinion, some way could not be found to prevent the drawing of the sword

Ulysses S. Grant

Airplanes are interesting toys, but of no military value

Ferdinand Foch

Gasoline spoils the character

Paul von Hindenburg

The machine gun is a much overrated weapon

Douglas Haig

SALES

Veni, vidi, vici (I came, I saw, I conquered)

Julius Caesar

There is no victory at bargain-basement prices

Dwight D. Eisenhower

Never arbitrate. Arbitration allows a third party to determine your destiny. It is the resort of the weak

Atilla the Hun

It is not sufficient that I suceed - all others must fail

Genghis Khan

I would rather be first in a village than second in Rome

Julius Caesar

The will to conquer is the first condition of victory

Ferdinand Foch

It is the success that makes great men

Napoleon Bonaparte

Success in battle depends mainly on morale and determination

Douglas Haig

So in war, the way is to avoid what is strong and to strike at what is weak

Sun Tzu

Nobody ever defended anything successfully, there is only attack and attack, and attack some more

George Patton Jr

The idea that a war can be won by standing on the defensive and waiting for the enemy to attack is a dangerous fallacy, one which owes its inception to the desire to evade the price of victory

Douglas Haig

COMPETITION

Wherever the enemy goes, let our troops go also

Ulysses S. Grant

War is the remedy that our enemies have chosen, and I say let us give them all they want

William Tecumseh Sherman

It is not these well-fed long-haired men that I fear, but the pale and the hungry-looking

Julius Caesar

I am not afraid of an army of lions led by a sheep; I am afraid of an army of sheep led by a lion

Alexander the Great

In a man-to-man fight, the winner is the one who puts an extra round in his magazine

Erwin Rommel

Do not underestimate the power of an enemy, no matter how great or small, to rise against you another day

Atilla the Hun

Prepare for war, since you have been unable to endure a peace

Scipio Africanus

I send you a kaffis of mustard seed, that you may taste and acknowledge the bitterness of my victory

Alexander the Great

May God have mercy upon my enemies, because I won't

George Patton Jr

Once you get them running, you stay right on top of them, and that way a small force can defeat a large one every time... Only thus can a weaker country cope with a stronger; it must make up in activity what it lacks in strength

Thomas 'Stonewall' Jackson

If they attack, we will defend. If they do not attack until winter comes, then we will and we will tear them to shreds!

Georgy Zhukov

I think it will surprise and
confound the enemy. They won't
know what I am about. It will
bring forward a pell-mell
battle, and that is what I want

Horatio Nelson

Experience teaches us that it is
much easier to prevent an enemy
from occupying a location than
it is to dislodge them after
they have taken possession

George Washington

A war is only lost if you have
lost it!

Erich von Manstein

Do not interfere with an army that is returning home. When you surround an army, leave an outlet free. Do not press a desperate foe too hard

Sun Tzu

Yesterday, at the beginning of the ground war, Iraq had the fourth-largest army in the world. Today they have the second-largest army in Iraq

H. Norman Schwarzkopf

The greatest happiness is to vanquish your enemies, to chase them before you, to rob them of their wealth, to see those dear to them bathed in tears, to clasp to your bosom their wives and daughters

Genghis Khan

CHAPTER 4.

Officers and management

An officer is a member of an armed force who holds a position of authority. Commissioned officers derive their authority directly from the sovereign and are charged with carrying out the duties and responsibilities of a specific office or position. In the field, an officer is in charge of non-commissioned officers and soldiers. In this chapter, we look at the similarities with management in the areas such as organizational skills, decision making, managing people and taking responsibility.

ORGANIZATIONAL SKILLS

Divide and conquer

Julius Caesar

The secret of all victory lies in the organization of the non-obvious

Marcus Aurelius

Only strength can cooperate. Weakness can only beg

Dwight D. Eisenhower

One minute can decide the outcome of a battle, one hour - the outcome of a campaign, and one day - the fate of a country

Aleksandr Vasilyevich Suvorov

Time is everything; five minutes can make the difference between victory and defeat

Horatio Nelson

Infantry must move forward to close with the enemy. It must shoot in order to move… To halt under fire is folly. To halt under fire and not fire back is suicide. Officers must set the example

George Patton Jr

Manoeuvring with an army is advantageous; with an undisciplined multitude, it is most dangerous

Sun Tzu

The difficulty of tactical manoeuvring consists in turning the devious into the direct, and misfortune into gain

Sun Tzu

The strength of an army is determined by the amount of automatic movements, measured by the number multiplied by the speed

Napoleon Bonaparte

Every change in the rules which impairs the principle weakens the army

William Tecumseh Sherman

An action committed in anger is an action doomed to failure

Genghis Khan

The sergeant is the Army

Dwight D. Eisenhower

No captain can do very wrong if he places his ship alongside that of the enemy

Horatio Nelson

Fighting with a large army under your command is nowise different from fighting with a small one: it is merely a question of instituting signs and signals

Sun Tzu

PROCESS THINKING

Nine times out of ten, an army has been destroyed because its supply lines have been severed

Douglas MacArthur

Success demands a high level of logistical and organizational competence

George Patton Jr

My rule was always to do the business of the day in the day

Duke of Wellington

DECISION MAKING

Alea iacta est ('The Die is Cast' - meaning that an important decision has been taken and that there is no turning back)

Julius Caesar

Decisions! And a general, a commander-in-chief who has not understood the importance of good decision making, is not a good commander

Montgomery

I mistrust the judgement of every man in a case which concerns his own wishes

Duke of Wellington

Few people think, and yet they all want to make decisions

Frederick the Great

Be firm in your decisions, you can weigh the pros and cons from before: but if your will is once declared, do not for anything in the world go back on it

Frederick the Great

When one is faced with the choice, it is better to be too sensitive than too hard

Frederick the Great

It takes less courage to criticize the decisions of others than to stand by your own

Atilla the Hun

MANAGING PEOPLE

Only those who have learned to obey can later command

Paul von Hindenburg

Diversity in council, unity in command

Cyrus the Great

Never give an order that cannot be obeyed

Douglas MacArthur

I cannot trust a man to control others who cannot control himself

Robert E. Lee

If you cannot get them to salute
when they should salute and
wear the clothes you tell them
to wear, how are you going
to get them to die for their
country?

George Patton Jr

Severity prevents more mistakes
than it represses

Napoleon Bonaparte

Great men are never cruel
without necessity

Napoleon Bonaparte

Never tell people how to do
things. Tell them what to do and
they will surprise you with
their ingenuity

George Patton Jr

Bestow rewards without regard to rule, issue orders without regard to previous arrangements; and you will be able to handle a whole army as though you had to do with but a single man

Sun Tzu

Don't say it's impossible! Then turn your command over to the next officer. If he cannot do it, I'll find someone who can, even if I have to take him from the ranks!

Thomas 'Stonewall' Jackson

An Army is a collection of armed men obliged to obey one man

William Tecumseh Sherman

We must encourage people rather than scare them off

Frederick the Great

If men make war in slavish obedience to rules, they will fail

Ulysses S. Grant

The leaders know exactly what is right for us

Erwin Rommel

I promoted you to a staff officer to let you know that you are not obedient

Frederick the Great

It is with rattles that men lead

Napoleon Bonaparte

Men are better governed through their vices than their virtues

Napoleon Bonaparte

You don't lead by hitting people over the head - that's assault, not leadership

Dwight D. Eisenhower

You are remembered for the rules you break

Douglas Macarthur

When I came to explain to them the Nelson Touch, it was like an electric shock. Some shed tears, all approved - it was new - it was singular - it was simple!

Horatio Nelson

I don't know what effect these men will have upon the enemy, but, by God, they terrify me

Duke of Wellington

Throw your soldiers into positions from whence there is no escape and they will prefer death to flight. If they will face death, there is nothing they may not achieve

Sun Tzu

JUDGEMENT AND ACCOUNTABILITY

To judge a man properly, one has to put oneself completely in the position in which he is

Frederick the Great

Our country will, I believe, sooner forgive an officer for attacking an enemy than for letting it alone

Horatio Nelson

It is better to offer no excuse than a bad one

George Washington

99% of failures come from people who make excuses

George Washington

And now it is the German generals who find it hard to explain away their retreat

Georgy Zhukov

I only want to be responsible to God, the Fatherland and my conscience

Paul von Hindenburg

TAKING RESPONSIBILITY

The eyes of the world are upon you. The hopes and prayers of liberty-loving people everywhere march with you

Dwight D. Eisenhower

The nature of encounter operations requires of commanders limitless initiative and constant readiness to take the responsibility for military actions

Georgy Zhukov

I am determined to defend the honour of the German Army!

Erich von Manstein

You could be the person who gives the orders that will bring about the deaths of thousands and thousands of young men and women. It is an awesome responsibility. You cannot fail. You dare not fail...

H. Norman Schwarzkopf

I yield to no man in sympathy for the gallant men under my command; but I am obliged to sweat them tonight, so that I may save their blood tomorrow

Thomas 'Stonewall' Jackson

A meeting to make a decision is odd, but three is too many

Ferdinand Foch

CHAPTER 5.

Army and careers

The military is a force for national security and for enforcing international law in certain emergency situations. The army is the part of that force that fights or operates primarily on land. Within an army, there have always been people who make it their career or profession, and this chapter looks at various aspects of that and its relevance to business today.

JOBS

When you put on a uniform there are certain inhibitions that you accept

Dwight D. Eisenhower

Every soldier must know, before he goes into battle, how the little battle he is to fight fits into the larger picture, and how the success of his fighting will influence the battle as a whole

Montgomery

War is hell - some of you young men think that war is all glamour and glory, but let me tell you, boys, it is all hell!

William Tecumseh Sherman

War to me is like a spa treatment

Paul von Hindenburg

There is a true glory and a true honour: the glory of duty done - the honour of the integrity of principle

Robert E. Lee

If my soldiers began to think, not one would remain in the ranks

Frederick the Great

Do not tell me that this problem is difficult. If it was easy, it would not be a problem

Ferdinand Foch

Execute every act of thy life as though it were thy last

Marcus Aurelius

The fact that I live is not important, but the fact that I work as long as I live

Frederick the Great

I hate war as only a soldier who has lived it can, as one who has seen its brutality, its futility, its stupidity

Dwight D. Eisenhower

Whoever is first in the field and awaits the coming of the enemy will be fresh for the fight; whoever is second in the field and has to hasten to battle will arrive exhausted

Sun Tzu

You can be busy without doing the slightest

Frederick the Great

The hardest thing of all for a soldier is to retreat

Duke of Wellington

Defeat is a common fate of a soldier and there is nothing to be ashamed of in it. The great point is whether we have performed our duty

Marquis Heihachiro Togo

We won the victory where it was easy to win and not over something that was hard to conquer... each division of the combined squadrons did its work well and not more. There was nothing remarkable in our bravery

Marquis Heihachiro Togo

I'm never less at leisure than when at leisure, or less alone than when alone

Scipio Africanus

I owe all my success in life to having always been a quarter of an hour beforehand

Horatio Nelson

The General hopes and trusts that every officer and man will endeavour to live and act as becomes a Christian soldier defending the dearest rights and liberties of his country

George Washington

Do your own reconnaissance. See for yourself and then get down to the job without delay

Erich von Manstein

No consideration may be powerful enough to cause an honest man to move away from his duty

Frederick the Great

A war is just like love, at the end someone has to leave by foot

Napoleon Bonaparte

DISCIPLINE

Discipline is the mother of victory

Aleksandr Vasilyevich Suvorov

Discipline is the soul of an army. It makes small numbers formidable, procures success to the weak, and esteem to all

George Washington

There is only one sort of discipline, perfect discipline

George Patton Jr

Discipline strengthens the mind so that it becomes impervious to the corroding influence of fear

Montgomery

CAREER

I had rather excel others in the knowledge of what is excellent, than in the extent of my power and dominion

Alexander the Great

Leadership consists of picking good men and helping them do their best

Chester W. Nimitz

I was well beaten myself, and I am better for it

Montgomery

Old soldiers never die; they just fade away

Douglas MacArthur

I cannot, if I am in the field
of glory, be kept out of sight:
wherever there is anything to
be done, there Providence is
sure to direct my steps

Horatio Nelson

I feel that retired generals
should never miss an
opportunity to remain silent
concerning matters for which
they are no longer responsible

H. Norman Schwarzkopf

It is now time to end the
anxiety of the Romans. Clearly
they are no longer able to wait
for the death of an old man who
has caused them so much concern

Hannibal

He who has the audacity to live the longest always learns something new

Frederick the Great

It is foolish and wrong to mourn the men who died. Rather we should thank God that such men lived

George Patton Jr

What is criminal is not to fail, it is lacking ambition

Napoleon Bonaparte

Age wrinkles the body. Quitting wrinkles the soul

Douglas MacArthur

TRAINING

Wise people learn when they can;
fools learn when they must

Duke of Wellington

There is no educated man;
there are only men who have
developed

Ferdinand Foch

Poverty, deprivation and misery
are the school of a good soldier

Napoleon Bonaparte

Learn from the things that have
been done already, for this is
the best way of learning

Cyrus the Great

The education of a man is never completed until he dies

Robert E. Lee

I have met, in my time, many an old fool; but this one* tops them all
(* said about the philosopher Phormio after he followed a lecture with him)

Hannibal

The Gods give the crown of victory to those who, by their training in peaceful times, are already victorious before they fight, and refuse it to those who, satisfied with one victory, rest contendedly in peace

Marquis Heihachiro Togo

In no other profession are the penalties for employing untrained personnel so appalling or so irrevocable as in the military

Douglas MacArthur

The cause of the recent victory of our navy, though it was in a great degree to the Imperial virtue, must also be attributed to our training in peaceful times which produced its fruits in war

Marquis Heihachiro Togo

COMMUNICATION

As-Salaam-Alaikum (an Arabic greeting meaning peace be unto you)

Saladin

Cadets can neither be treated as schoolboys or soldiers

Robert E. Lee

In general, men are quick to believe that which they wish to be true

Julius Caesar

To repay insult with insult is the way of the mob

Frederick the Great

Be discreet in all things, and so render it unnecessary to be mysterious about any

Duke of Wellington

He who reveals his intentions too early brings himself into danger because he gives his enemies time to take countermeasures.

Frederick the Great

I have only one eye, I have a right to be blind sometimes... I really do not see the signal!

Horatio Nelson

I never knew what to do with a paper except to put it in a side pocket or pass it to a clerk who understood it better than I did

Ulysses S. Grant

Luck and chance are two meaningless words

Frederick the Great

It is easier to bring certain people to talk than to let them be silent

Frederick the Great

COLLEAGUES

A true friend is a gift from heaven

Frederick the Great

Never do a wrong thing to make a friend - or to keep one

Robert E. Lee

For my friends, I would go through fire, and all that worries them would also touch me as if it concerned me

Frederick the Great

Be courteous to all, but intimate with few; and let those few be well tried before you give them your confidence

George Washington

I have come not to make war
on the Italians, but to aid the
Italians against Rome

Hannibal

Who could not conquer with such
troops as these?

Thomas 'Stonewall' Jackson

We love ourselves
notwithstanding our faults, and
we ought to love our friends in
like manner

Cyrus the Great

Grant stood by me when I was
crazy, and I stood by him when
he was drunk, and now we stand
by each other

William Tecumseh Sherman

Ours [our army] is composed of the scum of the earth - the mere scum of the earth

Duke of Wellington

There are different levels of humanity, but the duties of humanity are the same

Frederick the Great

I love treason but hate a traitor

Julius Caesar

What a cruel thing is war: to fill our hearts with hatred instead of love for our neighbours, and to devastate the fair face of this beautiful world

Robert E. Lee

All men have their frailties
and whoever looks for a friend
without imperfections will
never find what he seeks

Cyrus the Great

Et tu, Brute! (and you, Brutus!)*
(*Caesar's last words to his friend Marcus Brutus at the moment of his assassination; signifies the utmost betrayal)

Julius Caesar

There can be no greater error
than to expect or calculate
upon real favours from one
nation to another nation

George Washington

TEAM BUILDING

An army is a team. It lives, eats, sleeps, fights as a team. This individuality stuff is a bunch of bullshit

George Patton Jr

Remember upon the conduct of each depends the fate of all

Alexander the Great

The indulgences of which the people themselves are mutually guilty lead to tolerance

Frederick the Great

We cannot enter into alliances until we are acquainted with the designs of our neighbours

Sun Tzu

CHAPTER 6.

Soldiers and employees

The private soldier is the lowest rank in the army. Within the other armed forces of a country, the equivalent is sailor, airman or marine. This chapter covers aspects of the soldier such as courage, integrity, sacrifice and loyalty, all characteristics which apply to employees of successful organizations today.

CHARACTER

Obedience to lawful authority is the foundation of manly character

Robert E. Lee

Moral courage is the most valuable and usually the most absent characteristic in men

George Patton Jr

Real men despise battle, but will never run from it

George Washington

What counts is not necessarily the size of the dog in the fight - it's the size of the fight in the dog

Dwight D. Eisenhower

Dogs have all the good qualities of the people, without at the same time having their faults

Frederick the Great

All men are timid on entering any fight. Whether it is the first or the last fight, all of us are timid. Cowards are those who let their timidity get the better of their manhood

George Patton Jr

I hope I shall possess firmness and virtue enough to maintain what I consider the most enviable of all titles, the character of an honest man

George Washington

I have always acted on the principle of loyalty towards loyalty, trust to trust

Paul von Hindenburg

Honesty and gratitude are essential virtues without which people would be worse than wild beasts

Frederick the Great

Anger cannot be dishonest

Marcus Aurelius

The fault lies in the means much more than in the principles

Napoleon Bonaparte

Men are neither wholly good nor wholly bad, but possess and practise all that there is of good and bad here below

Napoleon Bonaparte

The confidence of the men in the ranks rests upon a man's strength of character

Erich von Manstein

There are only two powers in the world, the sword and the mind. In the long run, the sword is always defeated by the mind

Napoleon Bonaparte

Our armament must be adequate to the needs, but our faith is not primarily in these machines of defence but in ourselves

Chester W. Nimitz

To persevere in one's duty and be silent is the best answer to calumny*

(*the making of false and defamatory statements about someone in order to damage their reputation)

George Washington

INTEGRITY

It was not the applause of the world that was decisive in my life and doing, but my own convictions, the duty and conscience

Paul von Hindenburg

Never forget that your actions may become tradition

Paul von Hindenburg

A reasonable person should have nothing to do with abuse, not even with the truth

Frederick the Great

COURAGE

Courage is the overcoming of fear

Erwin Rommel

Courage is fear holding on a minute longer

George Patton Jr

There is much real courage needed to suffer with the constant punishment of the soul and remain fixed under the fire of a battery

Napoleon Bonaparte

True courage is being afraid, and going ahead and doing your job anyhow, that's what courage is

H. Norman Schwarzkopf

The more comfort the less courage there is

Aleksandr Vasilyevich Suvorov

Uncommon valour was a common virtue

Chester W. Nimitz

All men are frightened. The more intelligent they are, the more they are frightened

George Patton Jr

God has given to man no sharper spur to victory than contempt of death

Hannibal

EFFORT

A pint of sweat will save a gallon of blood

George Patton Jr

You must do your damnedest and win

George Patton Jr

Do your damnedest in an ostentatious manner all the time

George Patton Jr

When war does come, my advice is to draw the sword and throw away the scabbard

Thomas 'Stonewall' Jackson

It is fatal to enter any war
without the will to win it

Douglas MacArthur

Our greatest glory is not in
never falling, but in rising
every time we fall

Napoleon Bonaparte

Human happiness and moral duty
are inseparably connected

George Washington

Die for the Virgin, for your
mother the Empress, for the
royal family. The Church will
pray to God for the dead. The
survivor has honour and glory

Aleksandr Vasilyevich Suvorov

I don't give a damn about the colour of your skin, just kill as many sons of bitches wearing green as you can

George Patton Jr

The hardships of forced marches are often more painful than the dangers of battle

Thomas 'Stonewall' Jackson

… but for a soldier his duty is plain. He is to obey the orders of all those placed over him and whip the enemy wherever he meets him

Ulysses S. Grant

It is a fact that under equal conditions, large-scale battles and whole wars are won by troops who have a strong will for victory, clear goals before them, high moral standards, and devotion to the banner under which they go into battle

Georgy Zhukov

England expects that every man will do his duty

Horatio Nelson

Perseverance and spirit have done wonders in all ages

George Washington

Doing nothing is half death. Life manifests itself only in action

Frederick the Great

I am preparing for each event
that could come up. Whether
my luck is favourable or
unfavourable, that will make me
neither discouraged nor cocky

Frederick the Great

One must fight for his country
and fall, when you can save it,
and if not, it is an insult to
survive it

Frederick the Great

You have to want to live and
know how to die

Napoleon Bonaparte

You're never beaten until you
admit it

George Patton Jr

SACRIFICE

Just drive down that road, until you get blown up

George Patton Jr

I would not mind losing my sight if I took the city

Saladin

Reject your sense of injury and the injury itself disappears

Marcus Aurelius

Let me alone: I have yet my legs and one arm. Tell the surgeon to make haste with his instruments. I know I must lose my right arm, so the sooner it is off, the better

Horatio Nelson

The act of dying is one of the acts of life

Marcus Aurelius

VALUES AND NORMS

The soldier is valuable, more valuable than his own ego

Aleksandr Vasilyevich Suvorov

Duty is the great business of a sea officer; all private considerations must give way to it, however painful it may be

Horatio Nelson

A man will fight more for his interests than for his rights

Napoleon Bonaparte

With the German people we share the soldiers' inability to understand the true nature of the regime

Erich von Manstein

They have fought with you, they will share with you*
(*said as a response to the request of a South African officer not to be housed in the same barracks as his black subordinates)

Erwin Rommel

If a man consults whether he is to fight, when he has the power in his own hands, it is certain that his opinion is against fighting

Horatio Nelson

Few men have the virtue to withstand the highest bidder

George Washington

It is well that war is so terrible, or we should grow too fond of it

Robert E. Lee

We are not the master of our destiny. The whirlwind of events pulls us away and one is powerless against it

Frederick the Great

LOYALTY

Whoever fights against his country is a child who kills his mother

Napoleon Bonaparte

Loyalty is the mark of honour

Paul von Hindenburg

Loyalty is proven in times of tribulation, and loyalty is the mark of honour

Frederick the Great

The Field Marshal von Manstein will always remain loyal to the legal government

Erich von Manstein

True patriotism sometimes requires of men to act exactly contrary, at one period, to that which it does at another, and the motive which impels them the desire to do right is precisely the same

Robert E. Lee

I am unaware of any wrongdoing. I was not involved in any crime. I have only served my homeland, my whole life

Erwin Rommel

QUALITIES

The first quality of a soldier is constancy to endure the fatigue, the value is only secondary

Napoleon Bonaparte

Men recognize their own talents only after they have made the attempt to do this

Frederick the Great

Accustom yourself to tireless activity

Aleksandr Vasilyevich Suvorov

It is the part of a fool to say, I should not have thought that

Scipio Africanus

A general is just as good or just as bad as the troops under his command make him

Douglas MacArthur

If you are going to win any battle, you have to do one thing. You have to make the mind run the body. Never let the body tell the mind what to do… the body is never tired if the mind is not tired

George Patton Jr

I am a soldier, I fight where I am told, and I win where I fight

George Patton Jr

Watch what people are cynical about, and one can often discover what they lack

George Patton Jr

The clever combatant imposes his will on the enemy, but does not allow the enemy's will to be imposed on him

Sun Tzu

If you feel that the Chief of the General Staff talks only rubbish, my place is not here. Better to give me a command at the front where I can be of better use!

Georgy Zhukov

I could not tread these perilous paths in safety, if I did not keep a saving sense of humour

Horatio Nelson

Recollect that you must be a seaman to be an officer and also that you cannot be a good officer without being a gentleman

Horatio Nelson

A man's worth is no greater than the worth of his ambitions

Marcus Aurelius

FAMILY AND PRIVATE

The best luck of all is the luck you make for yourself

Douglas MacArthur

A moment of happiness outweighs millennia of posthumous fame

Frederick the Great

I am indebted to my father for living, but to my teacher for living well

Alexander the Great

In the environment in which I grew up, the world was Prussian soldiery

Erich von Manstein

Luxury drives man to no virtues - it usually smothers all the better feelings in him

Frederick the Great

No man is entitled to the blessings of freedom unless he be vigilant in its preservation

Douglas MacArthur

He who cannot stop drinking may get drunken three times a month. If he does it more often, he is guilty. To get drunken twice a month is better; once, still more praiseworthy. But not to drink at all - what could be better than this? But where could such a being be found? But if one could find him, he would be worthy of all honour

Genghis Khan

Go home all you boys who fought with me and help build up the shattered fortunes of our old state

Robert E. Lee

Do not suppose, my dearest sons, that when I have left you I shall be nowhere and no one. Even when I was with you, you did not see my soul, but knew that it was in this body of mine from what I did. Believe then that it is still the same, even though you see it not

Cyrus the Great

CHAPTER 7.
Victory and financial success

A military triumph or victory indicates that an army has won or been successful. This chapter equates victory in battle with financial success in business and looks at topics such as financial results, investments and risk management.

RESULTS

Power is an artist that I love

Napoleon Bonaparte

First gain the victory and then make the best use of it you can

Horatio Nelson

In war there is no substitute for victory

Douglas MacArthur

Today the victory had been the enemy's if there had been any one among them to gain it

Julius Caesar

The harder the conflict, the greater the triumph

George Washington

With stout hearts, and with enthusiasm for the contest, let us go forward to victory

Montgomery

If I win, I can't be stopped! If I lose I shall be dead

George Patton Jr

I want to impose on everyone that the bad times are over, they are finished! Our mandate from the Prime Minister is to destroy the Axis forces in North Africa... It can be done, and it will be done!

Montgomery

If you know the enemy and know yourself, your victory will not stand in doubt; if you know Heaven and know Earth, you may make your victory complete

Sun Tzu

It is the unconquerable nature of man and not the nature of the weapon he uses that ensures victory

George Patton Jr

The greatest danger lies in the moment of victory

Napoleon Bonaparte

If we lose the war in the air, we lose the war and we lose it quickly

Montgomery

Wars may be fought with weapons, but they are won by men. It is the spirit of the men who follow and of the man who leads that gains the victory

George Patton Jr

INVESTMENTS

A battery of field artillery is worth a thousand muskets

William Tecumseh Sherman

There's no smoke without fire

Georgy Zhukov

Shed sweat - but no blood

Erwin Rommel

Obviously, the greater the length of a war, the higher is likely to be the number of casualties in it on either side

Douglas Haig

A ship is always referred to as she because it costs so much to keep one in paint and powder

Chester W. Nimitz

Every gun that is made, every warship launched, every rocket fired, signifies in the final sense a theft from those who hunger and are not fed, those who are cold and are not clothed

Dwight D. Eisenhower

To define it rudely but not ineptly, engineering is the art of doing for ten shillings what any fool can do for a pound

Duke of Wellington

There is no security in this
life. There is only opportunity

Douglas MacArthur

Do not fight a battle if you do
not gain anything by winning

Erwin Rommel

About faith and hope the world
disagrees, but all mankind's
concern is charity

Alexander the Great

Worry is the interest paid by
those who borrow trouble

George Washington

One should never judge human
plans and activities by their
output

Frederick the Great

Liberty, when it begins to take root, is a plant of rapid growth

George Washington

The longer the battle lasts, the more force we will have to use!

Georgy Zhukov

SHAREHOLDERS

You carry Caesar and Caesar's fortune*
(*said by Julius Caesar to pirates who had captured him)

Julius Caesar

Wisdom is very likely to protect what you have, but only boldness understands the purchase

Frederick the Great

The rich take a hit, that is a necessity of war, but the poor, that is a disgrace

Napoleon Bonaparte

On the fields of friendly strife are sown the seed that on other days and other fields will bear the fruits of victory

Douglas MacArthur

The defeat of the combined French and Spanish fleets lifted the very real threat of an invasion of Britain and it was greeted by the nation with huge relief

Horatio Nelson

If my body dies, let my body die, but do not let my country die

Genghis Khan

RISK MANAGEMENT

How great are the dangers I face to win a good name in Athens

Alexander the Great

Chieftains must understand that the spirit of the law is greater than its letter

Atilla the Hun

If you must break the law, do it to seize power: in all other cases observe it

Julius Caesar

In war, you win or lose, live or die - and the difference is an eyelash

Douglas MacArthur

The US has broken the second rule of war. That is, do not go fighting with your land army on the mainland of Asia. Rule One is don't march on Moscow

Montgomery

The art of being sometimes very bold and sometimes very careful is the art of success

Napoleon Bonaparte

Take calculated risks

George Patton Jr

Desperate affairs require desperate measures

Horatio Nelson

Making no mistakes is what establishes the certainty of victory, for it means conquering an enemy that is already defeated

Sun Tzu

Is the proposed operation likely to succeed? What might the consequences of failure be? Is it in the realm of practicability in terms of material and supplies?

Chester W. Nimitz

If I had been censured every time I have run my ship, or fleets under my command, into great danger, I should have long ago been out of the Service and never in the House of Peers

Horatio Nelson

Hence that general is skilful in attack whose opponent does not know what to defend; and he is skilful in defence whose opponent does not know what to attack

Sun Tzu

The generals and warlords

Below is a brief description of all the generals and warlords in this book in chronological order.

Cyrus the Great (c.576 BC - 530 BC)
Cyrus II of Persia is one of the founders of the Persian Empire and was the first world leader to be referred to as 'the Great'. Cyrus led a revolt against the Medes and, as a result, became King of the Medes and Persians in 550 BC, an area which more or less coincides with the current region of Iran and eastern Turkey. His policies of conquest, mercifulness and assimilation were so successful that the empire continued to thrive for some 200 years after his death and his compassionate principles still resonate today.

Sun Tzu (c.544 BC - c.496 BC)
Sun Tzu was a Chinese general and author. 'Tzu' is an honorary title: his first name was Wu 武. It is believed that he was a general at the court of King Ho Lu of

the kingdom Wu. He is most famous for the book The art of war, which is accepted as a masterpiece on strategy and is frequently cited and referred to by generals and theorists even to this day.

Alexander the Great (356 BC - 323 BC)

Alexander III of Macedon was King of Macedonia and, at the age of 30, was the ruler of one of the largest empires in ancient times, an empire that stretched from the Ionian Sea to the Himalayas. In 334 BC, he attacked the Persian-controlled Anatolia (modern Turkey) region and subsequently conquered the entire Persian Empire. In an effort to reach the 'end of the world and the Great Outer Sea', he invaded India in 326 BC. Although he won the battle against the Indian prince, his troops refused to go any further due to the long months of tropical rainfall (monsoon).

Hannibal (247 BC - 183 BC)

Hannibal Barkas was a Carthaginian general (modern Tunisia). He was the main opponent of the Romans in the Second Punic War. With his army of some 50,000 soldiers, 8,000 horses and 37 elephants, he departed from Spain starting on a gruelling journey of over 2,400 kilometres to Italy. This famously included a section of some 200 kilometres through difficult terrain and on snowy mountain slopes to heights of over 2,750 metres. In Italy, he won many victories, but could not, or would not, besiege Rome itself. After 16 years of wandering in southern Italy, he was recalled empty-handed to Carthage where the Romans had formed an imminent threat. In 202 BC he was defeated at the Battle of Zama Regia.

Scipio Africanus (236 BC - 183 BC)
Publius Cornelius Scipio Africanus Maior was a Roman general in the Second Punic War in 210 BC. He is most famous for defeating Hannibal at the Battle of Zama Regia. He is seen as a military genius and was never defeated in battle. As a tribute to his victory over Carthage (Africa), the Senate gave him the agnomen, or nickname, 'Africanus'.

Julius Caesar (± 100 BC - 44 BC)
Gaius Julius Caesar was a Roman general who is best known for his conquest of Gaul. Gaul was the Roman name for a large area of western Europe, including France, Belgium and areas in Germany and the Netherlands to the west of the River Rhine. As a com-

mander, he promoted legionnaires based on ability and not on the basis of birth. He was also one of the first warlords who saw the engineers as part of warfare and his armies were sometimes known to have marched distances of up to 40 kilometres a day.

Marcus Aurelius (121 - 180)
Marcus Aurelius Antoninus Augustus reigned over the Roman Empire from 161 to 180. His first military action occurred in 166 when Germanic tribes invaded Italy, after which he returned to Rome in 169. He later fought again on the Germanic border and after a number of successful campaigns in Germania in 172 he received the title Germanicus. In Rome today, at the Piazza Colonna, there is a column bearing the statue of Marcus Aurelius that has been there since ancient times.

Atilla the Hun (406 - 453)
Attila the Hun was the ruler of the Huns from 433 until his death. The Empire of the Huns stretched from the Urals (Russia) to the Rhine. During his reign, he was one of the most feared enemies of both the Western and the Eastern Roman Empire. He conducted several field trips out to the West and even stood

at the gates of Paris. Today his name remains associated with brutality and cruelty.

Saladin (1137 - 1193)

Salah ad-Din Yusuf ibn Ayyub was a Syrian general who founded the Ayyubid dynasty of Egypt and Syria. In 1174, Saladin was Sultan of Egypt and later, in 1181, of Syria. His most famous act was the capture of Jerusalem from the Crusaders by first defeating a large army of Christians (between 15,000 and 20,000 soldiers) during the Battle of Hattin in 1187, after which he was able to take the city in the same year.

Genghis Khan (1162 - 1227)

Genghis Khan was a Mongol warlord. He united the Mongol tribes and eventually conquered a large part of modern Asia and laid the foundation for the formation of a new empire, the second largest in history, stretching from China to the Danube River (Romania). For one large-scale attack on western China, he once gathered an army of as many as 200,000 men. He also has a reputation for cruelty and for the plundering of towns.

Frederick the Great (24 January 1712 - 17 August 1786)

Frederick II was a German warlord and King of the state of Prussia. He expanded his principality during the Austrian War of Succession (1740-1748) and fought in the Seven Years' War (1756-1763) against France, Russia, Bohemia and Saxony Electorate. In 1772, he managed to annex, through a diplomatic route, West Prussia, and in 1778-1779, he prevented parts of Bavaria from becomng part of Austria.

Suvorov (24 November 1729 - 18 May 1800)

Aleksandr Vasilyevich, Count Suvorov, was a Russian general who, because he never lost a battle, is seen as one of the really great men in military history. He played an important role In the Russo-Turkish War of 1787-1792. After the war, he was in charge of the campaign in Poland, and in 1794 he managed to take Warsaw. In 1799 he became head of the Russian army that fought in Italy against the French. Although he was able to achieve some victories, he had to flee and had to cross the Alps in order to be able to regroup his army. For this tactic Suvorov received the never-before-granted rank of Generalissimo. In a number of countries, Generalissimo is the highest military rank.

George Washington (22 February 1732 - 14 December 1799)

George Washington was an American general who, in 1775, was elected to be the commander-in-chief of the colonial forces during the American War of Independence. The turning point in this war was the Battle of Yorktown where, together with French troops, he defeated the British. In 1783, Britain recognized American independence.

Horatio Nelson (29 September 1758 - 21 October 1805)

Horatio Nelson, Viscount Nelson, Duke of Bronte, was a British admiral and is best known for his victory at the Battle of Trafalgar in 1805 against the French and Spaniards in which he triumphed even though it cost him his own life. This victory ensured that the British Empire became dominant in all the oceans of the world. As a tribute, he was given a state funeral and buried in St Paul's Cathedral in London.

Napoleon Bonaparte (15 August 1769 - 5 May 1821)

Napoleon was a French soldier who is known for the conquest of large parts of continental Europe as a result of the eponymous Napoleonic wars. The Russian campaign in 1812 marked the turning point of his rule and in 1814 he was forced to abdicate and was exiled. Less than ten months later, he managed to escape and came back to power. He was finally defeated at Waterloo in 1815.

Duke of Wellington (1 May 1769 - 14 September 1852)

Arthur Wellesley, 1st Duke of Wellington, was an Irish general in British service. He is most well known for the Battle of Waterloo (1815) where he defeated Napoleon after his return from Elba. Previously, he had the French expelled out of Portugal and Spain, and defeated them at the Battle of Toulouse. Four days earlier, Napoleon had abdicated. The traditional dish 'Beef Wellington' is named after him.

Robert Lee (19 January 1807 - 12 October 1870)

Robert Edward Lee was an American general of the Southern troops during the Civil War and in 1862 became the commander-in-chief. Initially, he was successful against the much larger Northern armies, but the turning point in the civil war came with his defeat at Gettysburg in 1863.

William Sherman (8 February 1820 - 14 February 1891)

William Tecumseh Sherman was an American general of the Union troops during the Civil War. He is most famous for his capture of the City of Atlanta and his March to the Sea (from Atlanta to Savannah). Historians have recognized him for his military strategy as well as criticizing him for his 'scorched earth' policy.

Ulysses Grant (27 April 1822 - 23 July 1885)

Ulysses Simpson Grant is the most famous northern general from the American Civil War. In 1862, he won the first major victory for the North at Fort Henry in Tennessee. He was tenacious and willing to bear huge losses, while from his opponents he demanded unconditional surrender, which led to his nickname, 'Unconditional Surrender Grant'. In 1864, he was given command of all the troops of the United States. After the Civil War, he was the first so-called 'General of the Army' or five-star general.

'Stonewall' Jackson (21 January 1824 - 10 May 1863)

Thomas Jonathan Jackson was an American general with the Confederate forces during the American

Civil War. Here, historians praise his Shenandoah Valley field trips and encirclement of the Northern right wing at Chancellorsville, while his weaker performances are seen as being during the battles around Richmond. His nickname, Stonewall, comes from his performance during the first Battle of Bull Run, where he led the troops themselves and regardless of the enemy fire, he remained standing rock solid.

Heihachiro Togo (27 January 1848 - 30 May 1934)
Marquis Heihachiro Togo was a Japanese admiral who is famous for his victory over the Russian fleet at the Battle of Tsushima. The Battle of Tsushima was the decisive naval battle of the Russo-Japanese War (1904-1905). He is also called the Nelson of the East because of more or less using the same tactics employed by Nelson at the Battle of Trafalgar.

Paul von Hindenburg (2 October 1847 - 2 August 1934)
Paul von Hindenburg was a German general with the rank of Field Marshal. He had been retired for three years before he was called back to take part in the First World War. His victory over the Russians at the Battle of Tannenberg in 1914 instantly made him a national hero. In 1916 he became Germany's Chief of

the General Staff and was later to become President of Germany.

Ferdinand Foch (2 October 1859 - 20 March 1929)
Ferdinand Foch was a French general during the First World War. In the last year of the war, he was appointed Commander of the Allied Forces and Marshal of the French troops. During the surrender negotiations, he advocated peace terms that would mean that Germany would never again form a threat to France. After the Treaty of Versailles, he prophetically declared: 'This is not peace, it is an armistice for twenty years'.

Douglas Haig (19 June 1861 - 29 January 1928)
Douglas Haig was a British general during the First World War, and from 1915, the British Commander in Chief. He remains somewhat controversial because some historians believe that he took large losses for granted and made little or no use of the latest military technologies.

Douglas MacArthur (26 January 1880 - 5 April 1964)
Douglas MacArthur was an American general and commander of American forces in the Far East during

the Second World War. In 1944 he received the rank of General of the Army. He led the United Nations Command in the Korean War until he was controversially removed from command by President Harry S. Truman on 11 April 1951. He is currently only one of five American 'five-star' generals in the history of USA.

Chester Nimitz (24 February 1885 - 20 February 1966)
Chester William Nimitz was an American admiral who led the American fleet in the Pacific Ocean during the Second World War. In 1944 he was promoted to fleet admiral. The Japanese surrender was signed aboard his flagship, the USS Missouri.

George Patton (11 November 1885 - 21 December 1945)

George Smith Patton Jr was an American general who became famous during the Second World War for his crackdown against his troops and his successful relief operations during the Battle of the Bulge. In 1943 he was given command of the 2nd Army Corps in North Africa (Morocco) and pushed the German troops back to the east. After landing at Normandy, he was responsible for the right wing of the ground troops and later spearheaded the advance in Germany. He became known by his troops as 'Old Blood and Guts'.

Montgomery (17 November 1887 - 24 March 1976)

Bernard Law Montgomery, 1st Viscount Montgomery of Alamein, was a British general and Field Marshal. In late 1942 he was responsible for the first major offensive victory by the British against the Germans in North Africa and, from that moment on, the German army was increasingly driven back, leading in 1943 to the end of the German and Italian presence in North Africa. After landing at Normandy, he was responsible for the liberation of the Netherlands and the conquest of the north of Germany. Montgomery was known to his troops as 'Monty'.

Erich von Manstein (24 November 1887 - 9 June 1973)

Erich von Manstein was a German general who was appointed to the rank of Field Marshal in 1942. He came from an aristocratic Prussian family with a long military history and was regarded as one of the best German military strategists and commanders in the field during the Second World War. In March 1944 von Manstein was relieved from his post because of a difference of opinion with the Führer on which strategy to pursue on the Eastern Front.

Dwight Eisenhower (14 October 1890 - 28 March 1969)

Dwight David Eisenhower was an American five-star general during the Second World War and served as Supreme Commander of the Allied forces in Europe. He was responsible for planning and supervising Operation Torch, the invasion of North Africa in 1942-1943, and the successful invasion of France and Germany in 1944-1945. He later became the 34th President of the United States of America.

Erwin Rommel (15 November 1891 - 14 October 1944)

Erwin Johannes Eugen Rommel was a German general during the Second World War and earned the respect of both his own troops and those of his enemies. He is known for his leadership of the German and Italian forces in the North African campaign, which earned him the nickname, 'Desert Fox'. He is remembered as a humane and professional officer. His Afrika Korps was never accused of any war crimes, and soldiers captured during the Africa campaign reported humane treatment. Furthermore, he ignored any orders to kill Jewish soldiers, civilians and captured commandos.

Georgy Zhukov (1 December 1896 - 18 June 1974)

Georgy Konstantinovich Zhukov was a Soviet general who was appointed Marshal of the Soviet Union in 1943. In 1941 he had successfully defended Leningrad, now St Petersburg, against the Germans, and later that same year, Moscow. He led the Red Army in the liberation of his country and most of eastern Europe, and eventually conquered Berlin. He is the most decorated officer in the history of the Soviet Union and Russia.

H. Norman Schwarzkopf Jr (22 August 1934 - 27 December 2012)

Herbert Norman Schwarzkopf was an American general who led the coalition forces, an international force comprising more than 750,000 troops, in the first Gulf War (Operation Desert Storm) in 1990. He was also involved in the American invasion of Grenada in 1983. Schwarzkopf is considered an exceptional leader by biographers and is regarded for his abilities as a military diplomat and in dealing with the press.

Sources and accountability

The following sources were among those consulted:
- 1001.votes.com
- allzitate.de
- aphorismen.de
- benoa.net
- brainquote.com
- goodreads.com
- izquotes.com
- military-quotes.com
- quoteid.com
- thinkexist.com
- Tsouras, P.G. (2005), Dictionary of Military Quotations, Greenhill Books, London

Quotations of ancient times are difficult to attribute definitively and it is possible that some of these were linked to the respective general or warlord at a later time.

Other titles in this series

Nautical expressions for managers

"Future titles"
Biblical expressions for managers
Sport expressions for managers